The Practice of Journaling Prayer, Testimony, and Gratitude

EXPANDED EDITION

Stephanie M. Fletcher-Lartey

The Practice of Journaling Prayer, Testimony, and Gratitude
by Stephanie Mahalia Fletcher-Lartey
© Copyright 2024 Stephanie Mahalia Fletcher-Lartey - All rights reserved.

ISBN 978-0-6454846-2-5

No part of this book in either electronic means or printed format may be reproduced or used in any manner without the prior written permission of the copyright owner, except for the use of brief quotations in a book review or similar article.

Unless otherwise noted, all Scripture quotations are taken from the Holy Bible, English Standard Version (ESV). Copyright "2001 by Crossway Bibles, a division of Good News Publishers. Used by permission. All rights reserved.

The Practice of Journaling Prayer, Testimony, and Gratitude

Contents

About the Author	1

About this Book

Preface	5
1 The Practice of Spiritual Journaling	7
2 Historical Perspectives on Spiritual Journaling	14
3 The Science of The Spiritual Practices: prayer, testimony, and gratitude	19
4 Real-Life Testimonials: The Transformative Power of Journaling	24
5 Journaling Prayer, Testimony, and Gratitude	28
6 Journaling Your Prayers	32
7 Journaling Your Gratitude	41
8 Journaling Your Testimony	51

9
Maintaining Motivation for Your Journal — 57

10
Exploring Various Formats of Journaling — 68

11
Making Your Own Journal — 71

12
Further Reading and Resources — 75

Expanded Journaling Prompts — 78

Bibliography — 101

About the Author

Dr. Stephanie Mahalia Fletcher-Lartey is a multifaceted professional with a passion for empowering others. As a Christian pastor, she brings spiritual insight and compassion to her work. Her expertise extends beyond the pulpit, as she is an expert advisor on various public health topics, an advocate for application of kingdom principles in the marketplace, and a transformation coach.

Dr. Fletcher-Lartey's life journey is marked by diverse experiences. Her background as an international public health specialist and epidemiologist, informs her holistic approach to well-being and ministry. Through her research, writing, and community engagement, she advocates for building individual capacity to overcome limiting beliefs and paradigms, towards building spiritual and mental resilience. She is the author of *The Professional Believer's Guide: Principles to help believers thrive in the marketplace*, a tremendous resource for people looking for effective strategies to live a God-honouring life.

In this new book, "*The Practice of Journaling Prayer, Testimony, and Gratitude*," Dr. Stephanie Fletcher-Lartey shares practical wisdom on cultivating a transformative practice of spiritual journaling. She applies her deep understanding of the spiritual practices of prayer, gratitude and testimony and how to further cultivate them through the application of journaling. Whether you are seeking spiritual connection, personal growth, or emotional healing, her insights will guide you toward a richer, more intentional spirit-filled life.

Join Dr. Fletcher-Lartey on this journey of self-discovery. Through her words, you will find encouragement, authenticity, and a pathway to deeper purpose.

About this Book

Journaling is a powerful spiritual practice that enriches our faith journey. *"The Practice of Journaling Prayer, Testimony, and Gratitude,"* provides practical wisdom on cultivating a transformative practice of spiritual journaling. This is a companion book to the *"Prayer, Testimony and Gratitude Journal."*

In this book, you are invited to deepen your understanding of the spiritual discipline of journaling. It provides practical and theoretical insights to help you deepen your understanding about prayer, gratitude and testimony, as spiritual, life-giving practices. The book encourages one to build their relationship with God, celebrate His faithfulness, and cultivate a heart of gratitude.

The book has thirteen chapters. The first three chapters introduce the practice, history and science of spiritual journaling, its importance, and benefits. This is followed by an introduction to the practice of journaling prayer, testimony, and gratitude, as three important spiritual practices, with a chapter dedicated to each of these practices. Insights on overcoming pitfalls and maintaining motivation during the journaling process and practice are also included. It ends with some practical tips to explore different journal formats and how to make your own do-it-yourself (DIY) journal. Some additional reading material is referenced as well. The final section is a dedicated space where expanded journaling prompts have been provided where you can begin to practice the art of journaling, whether it is on special occasions or to celebrate, document prayers, gratitude and testimonies or just to make a note of key milestones.

Use this guide to support your journey in the practice of spiritual journaling, as you develop the habit of journaling through the lens of the Word of God.

"I pray that the eyes of your heart may be enlightened in order that you may know the hope to which he has called you, the riches of his glorious inheritance in his holy people." Ephesians 1:18

Preface

The Sacred Ledger - A Companion Through Time

In quiet chambers of the heart, Where silence weaves its sacred art, I wield my pen, a seeker's tool, chronicling life's journey long after school.

Prayers unfurl like fragile wings, Seeking solace in whispered things, Testimonies etched in ink's embrace, cementing God's goodness in history's embrace..

Gratitude spills from every line, thankfulness abound, a gift of time, Leather-bound or digital, it matters not, For journaling hits my soul's sweet spot.

Documenting dreams, life's happenings or scientific trends, it matters not the subject, the truth transcends, What I do is second nature, true, A dance of words—a lifelong cue.

So as the pages turn, And ink trails lead to stories untold, For within these lines, a writers pen tap, Etching prayers, thanksgiving and testimonies onto a sacred map.

Poem by Stephanie Fletcher-Lartey

Journaling has always been a part of my life. In the quiet moments, when the world hushes its clamor, I reach for my journal. Its pages, like a faithful companion, hold my thoughts, dreams, and reflections. As an epidemiologist and researcher, I document data meticulously— observations, words, charts, graphs, statistical analyses—but my personal journal transcends the clinical precision of my profession. It is a transformational practice of spiritual journaling that shapes my communication with the Divine.

Prayer: My pen dances across the paper, weaving prayers into existence. I write to the Divine, pouring out my hopes, fears, and gratitude. These whispered conversations bridge the gap between the earthly and the ethereal, anchoring me in purpose.

Testimony: Each sermon, every whispered revelation, finds its place in ink. I record moments of illumination, the echoes of truth that resonate within. These testimonies become steppingstones, guiding me through life's labyrinth.

Gratitude: Gratitude is my compass. I chronicle sunrises, the warmth of a friend's smile, the scent of rain-soaked earth. These fragments of joy accumulate, forming a mosaic of thanksgiving. Gratitude is the heartbeat of my days.

The leather-bound journals that line my shelves are a tangible map of my journey through the years. They bear witness to seasons of transition, growth, loneliness, heartache, triumph, and wonder. With the dawn of the digital age, my phone is a worthy companion that now captures snippets of my existence: an idea, thought, answered prayers, prophetic insights, a fleeting sunset, a child's laughter, a reminder to call a forgotten friend, or the words of the still small Voice. The medium changes, but the essence remains.

Journaling has been and remains my sanctuary, where science and faith intertwine. It forms part of the rhythm of my days, the solace in my nights. What I do is second nature—a sacred practice that stitches together the fabric of my professional and spiritual life. As you read this book, I invite you to join me on this transformational journey and experience a deeper connection and relationship with the Divine, through your practice of prayer, gratitude and testimony.

1

The Practice of Spiritual Journaling

Spiritual journaling is a practice that involves reflecting on your spiritual journey, exploring your inner thoughts and feelings, and connecting with yourself on a deeper soul level. Spiritual journaling involves recording your thoughts, prayers, activities, and experiences related to your daily life and spiritual journey with God. It is a way to reflect on Scripture and deepen your faith. You can keep a journal in either a physical notebook or an electronic format. Spiritual journaling from a Christian perspective, serves the purpose of fostering spiritual growth. Journaling is considered a spiritual discipline.

From a Christian perspective, spiritual discipline refers to regularly repeated practices that enrich our attentiveness to the Holy Spirit, cultivate the life and character of Jesus Christ within us, and strengthen our love for God and others. These transformative practices equip us to better serve God and our neighbours. Widely known examples of spiritual disciplines include Bible reading, prayer, meditation, worship, fasting, solitude, fellowship, and acts of service. However, the spectrum of faith-formative activities extends beyond these. In her accessible "Spiritual Disciplines Handbook," Adele Calhoun introduces 60 diverse faith practices, including discernment, unity, and teachability. They help us draw closer to God, align our lives with His will, and deepen our faith.

When approached intentionally, journaling becomes a sacred practice that fosters self-reflection, prayer, and connection with God. By recording your thoughts, prayers, and experiences, you create a space for spiritual growth and deeper understanding.

Many famous historical figures, including saints, artists, and thinkers, have kept journals. Some notable examples include:

- **Leonardo da Vinci**: The genius behind artistic masterpieces like the Mona Lisa and The Last Supper. His journals contain sketches, scientific observations, and philosophical musings. Approximately 7,000 pages survive, revealing his brilliant mind.
- **St. Therese of Lisieux**: Known for her spiritual autobiography, "The Story of a Soul." Her journal reflects her "Little Way" of seeking holiness through small acts of love and devotion.
- **St. Ignatius Loyola**: Founder of the Jesuits, maintained a journal that is famous for forming the basis for the "Spiritual Exercises," a renowned guide to spiritual growth and discernment.
- **St. Faustina Kowalska**: Author of the "Diary of Saint Maria Faustina Kowalska." Her writings focus on the message and devotion to the Divine Mercy.[vi]
- **Ludwig van Beethoven, Benjamin Franklin**, and others: These historical figures also kept journals, documenting their thoughts, experiences, and creative processes.

The journals kept by many of these world renown figures provide glimpses into their inner lives, struggles, and profound spiritual journeys.

Importance of Spiritual Journaling

Spiritual journaling is important for various reasons.

Self-Reflection: Self-reflection is a powerful practice that helps you understand yourself better, fostering personal growth and well-being.

Self-reflection contributes to your self-concept—the thoughts you have about your traits, abilities, beliefs, values, roles, and relationships. By reflecting inward, you get to know yourself better as you evolve over time. Strengthening your self-concept enhances your identity and influences your mood and behaviour. Self-reflection is essential for personal growth and development. Evaluate your strengths, weaknesses, and past actions. For instance, if a presentation did not go well, reflect on why. It could be, that you did not practice enough. Recognizing areas for improvement empowers you to make positive changes. Journaling allows you to pause, introspect, and gain insights into your spiritual growth. By putting your thoughts on paper, you can identify patterns, challenges, and moments of clarity.

Dialogue with God: Spiritual journaling serves as a powerful way to dialogue with God. When you write in your spiritual journal, you create a space for heartfelt communication with your Creator. The journal can be treated as a direct conversation with God. Instead of starting out with "Dear Diary," address Him as "Dear Jesus" or "Good evening/day/night Lord." This acts as a reminder that you are not just venting about life but that you are in prayerful dialogue with the Master. Each journal entry can be focused on a specific theme or situation. Whether it is a prayer, a testimony, a thanksgiving, or gratitude, use this heart posture to guide your conversation with God. Honesty and Authenticity are important when communicating with God. It is important to be honest about your experiences, feelings, and desires, as you journal. God desires our true selves—walls down, hearts open, as this helps to foster a deeper relationship.

Just as prayer is a conversation with God, journaling becomes a written dialogue. You express your heart's desires, questions, and struggles, inviting God to respond through His Word and Spirit.

Renewal and Healing: Spiritual journaling is a powerful practice that brings renewal and healing to your emotional and spiritual life. Writing about your experiences allows you to explore your feelings in a safe environment. This facilitates emotional release and closure, leading to healing. As you pay attention to your thoughts and feelings, you hold them up to the truth of God's Word. This process leads to renewal and healing as you align your perspective with His.

As you journal, you gain clarity on your thoughts, fears, and hopes. The process of reflection produces insights emerge, helping you understand yourself better and find meaning in life's chaos. Reading over previous journal entries, can help you witness growth and transformation, as you experience renewed perspectives that enables you to move forward with hope and purpose.

A Record of Your Journey: Your journal becomes a spiritual ledger, documenting your walk with God, as you regularly write down your prayers, reflections, and encounters with God, documenting both highs and lows—moments of joy, doubts, gratitude, and growth. Timestamping your journal entries allows you to track your progress over time, and consequently, you can observe recurring themes or lessons, answered prayers, and spiritual milestones. These can even be insights from Scripture, sermons, or personal revelations during time spent with God. Over time, you will see how He works in your life, celebrates victories, and comforts you during challenges.

Biblical and Historical Roots: Journaling as a spiritual discipline has biblical and historical roots. The Bible itself serves as an extensive journal, capturing divine encounters between biblical authors and God. God encourages people to document and write their visions. In Habakkuk 2:2, God instructs, "*Write the vision; make it plain on tablets.*" Early Christian figures like Saint Augustine and Julian of Norwich also kept detailed writings of their prayers and spiritual experiences. Journaling facilitates personal introspection and divine communication.

Journaling provides an opportunity to express our innermost thoughts and feelings to God. Through journaling, as we pay attention to our emotions, we hold them up to the truth of God's Word, experiencing renewal and healing.[xv] There are several Scriptural References that can be used as a guide:

- Begin your journaling with intentional focus on God's presence (e.g., Psalm 100, Revelation 3:20).

- Write honestly about your heart's issues, seeking God's perspective (e.g., Psalm 69, 137, 21, 30).
- Listen for God's voice through Scripture (1 Samuel 3:10).
- Confess sin and embrace God's compassion (Psalm 103:8-14, 1 John 1:9, Romans 8:1).
- Praise and worship God (focus on His attributes) to lift your perspective beyond circumstances.

Tangible Expressions of Your Walk with God: Your prayer journal becomes a tangible manifestation of your faith journey. It is a space for unguarded communication with God, where you can express hopes, fears, gratitude, and reflections. As you revisit your entries, you will see how God works in your life over time.[xiv]

A one-size-fits-all approach does not work with spiritual journaling. It is important to choose a journal that resonates with you, find a quiet space, and be intentional. Harness your creativity - whether through written words or art, and let your journal be a sacred space for growth and connection.

Spiritual Benefits of Journaling

Journaling is a powerful spiritual practice that enriches our faith journey. Whether you are writing down prayers, recording testimonies, or expressing gratitude, journaling offers profound benefits, such as:

Deepens Relationship with God:

- Conversing with God: Your journal becomes a sacred space for heartfelt conversations with the Divine.

- Reflecting on Scripture: Document insights from your Bible readings and meditations.
- Connecting with Yourself: Explore inner thoughts and feelings.

Tracks Spiritual Progress:

- Record of Growth: Over time, your journal becomes a record of your spiritual journey.
- Recognizing God's Work: Revisit past entries to see how God has shaped your life.

Reveals God's Communication:

- Divine Guidance: As you write, you become attuned to God's voice and leading.
- Messages and Insights: Record visions, dreams, and verses that resonate with you.

Archives Testimonies:

- God's Faithfulness: Document answered prayers, blessings, and moments of divine intervention.
- Encouragement: Reading past testimonies fuels your faith during challenging times.

Cements Your Relationship with God:

- Habit of Seeking: Regular journaling draws you closer to God.
- Shift of Focus: As you write, your attention shifts from self to the Almighty.

Fosters Gratitude:

- Thankfulness: Cultivate gratitude by listing daily blessings.

- Worship: Expressing gratitude becomes an act of worship.

Improves Prayer Life:

- Organized Prayers: Writing down prayers enhances your prayer experience.
- Intentionality: Reflect on your requests and conversations with God.

Discerns God's Voice and Direction:

- Fine-Tuning: Journaling helps you recognize God's truth and perspective.
- Holistic Self-Care: It promotes well-being by grounding you in Scripture.

When it comes to journaling, there's no one-size-fits-all approach. So, whether you express yourself through written words or art, your journal should be a sacred companion on your spiritual journey. Get excited as you begin to journal today and watch how your discipline through journaling enriches your spiritual journey and growth.

Reflection

What did you learn? How can/ will you apply what you have learned to your personal life?

2

Historical Perspectives on Spiritual Journaling

Many famous historical figures, including saints, artists, and thinkers, have kept journals. Some notable examples include:

- **Leonardo da Vinci:** The genius behind artistic masterpieces like the Mona Lisa and The Last Supper. His journals contain sketches, scientific observations, and philosophical musings. Approximately 7,000 pages survive, revealing his brilliant mind.
- **Therese of Lisieux:** Known for her spiritual autobiography, "The Story of a Soul." Her journal reflects her "Little Way" of seeking holiness through small acts of love and devotion.
- **Ignatius Loyola:** Founder of the Jesuits maintained a journal that is famous for forming the basis for the "Spiritual Exercises," a renowned guide to spiritual growth and discernment.
- **Faustina Kowalska:** Author of the "Diary of Saint Maria Faustina Kowalska." Her writings focus on the message and devotion to the Divine Mercy.vi
- **Ludwig van Beethoven, Benjamin Franklin**, and others: These

historical figures also kept journals, documenting their thoughts, experiences, and creative processes.

The journals kept by many of these world renown figures provide glimpses into their inner lives, struggles, and profound spiritual journeys.

Biblical Authors and Journaling

Early Recording of Divine Encounters

The practice of documenting spiritual encounters and divine revelations is evident throughout the Bible. Many of the biblical authors can be seen as spiritual journalists who recorded their direct experiences with God, their prayers, and reflections. In fact, one may even describe the Bible as a compilation or anthology consisting of the journals of numerous authors. The fervent and habitual practice of journaling spiritual encounters, divine revelations, prayers, poetry, words of wisdom and historical perspectives of the chosen family, has significantly shaped the biblical canon (the scriptural books that God has given his people, distinguished by divine qualities, church reception, and apostolic connection), as we know it today.

The Psalms: A Collection of Spiritual Reflections

The Book of Psalms is one of the most prominent examples of spiritual journaling in the Bible. Authored predominantly by King David, the Psalms are a collection of songs, prayers, and reflections that express a wide range of emotions, from profound despair to ecstatic praise. David's heartfelt journaling has provided comfort, guidance, and inspiration to believers for centuries.

Prophetic Writings

The prophets of the Old Testament, such as Isaiah, Jeremiah, and Ezekiel, recorded their visions, divine messages, and personal reflections. These writings were not only a direct response to their encounters with God but also served as a historical journal of Israel's relationship with the divine. For instance, Jeremiah's "Lamentations" captures his deep anguish and prophetic insight into the fall of Jerusalem. Isaiah's writings document detailed and extensive revelations of God's plan to come into the world in human form, to save the world.

The Gospels: Reflective Narratives

The four Gospels of the New Testament—Matthew, Mark, Luke, and John—can also be seen as forms of spiritual journaling. The authors documented the life, teachings, and miracles of Jesus Christ, each from their own perspective. These texts not only preserve the historical events but also provide intimate insights into the spiritual significance of Jesus' ministry.

Luke, in particular, is noteworthy for his meticulous approach. As both a physician and a historian, Luke's Gospel and his follow-up work, the Acts of the Apostles, offer detailed accounts, which were likely compiled from his personal reflections and interviews with eyewitnesses, thus functioning as a spiritual journal of the early Christian movement.

The Epistles: Letters of Guidance and Reflection

The Epistles, written by apostles such as Paul, Peter, James, and John, are profound examples of spiritual journaling in the form of letters. Paul's epistles, for example, are filled with theological reflections, personal experiences, and guidance for early Christian communities. His letters often contain passionate prayers and reflections on his mission, struggles, and relationship with Christ.

The Book of Revelation

John's Revelation can be considered as a vivid and symbolic journal of visions he experienced while on the island of Patmos. This eschatological book records John's prophetic visions and is a profound spiritual document that has influenced Christian eschatology and theology.

Early Christian Traditions

Spiritual journaling has deep roots in early Christian traditions.

Monastic communities often kept spiritual journals as part of their daily practice. One notable figure is Saint Augustine of Hippo, whose "Confessions" is considered one of the earliest examples of spiritual autobiography, blending personal reflection with theological insights.

Medieval Mysticism

During the medieval period, mystics like Hildegard of Bingen and Julian of Norwich documented their visions and spiritual experiences. Hildegard's writings, which include her journals, enriched the understanding of divine visions and their impact on personal faith and community life. Julian's "Revelations of Divine Love" remains a profound piece of spiritual literature, offering insight into her mystical experiences and reflections on God's love.

Reformation and Enlightenment

In the Reformation era, figures like Martin Luther and John Wesley emphasized personal faith and introspection. John Wesley is considered one of the most influential figures of the Great Awakening and the explosive revivals leading to modern evangelicalism. John Wesley, the founder of Methodism, kept detailed spiritual journals, which played a significant role in the development of Methodism. Wesley's journals not only documented his spiritual experiences but also his evangelical travels and the growth of the Methodist movement. His journal provides valuable insights into his thoughts, struggles, and encounters with God, making it a rich resource for understanding his impact on Christianity.

Eastern Traditions

Eastern religious traditions also hold a rich history of spiritual journaling. In Buddhism, Zen monks often keep written records of their meditative experiences and spiritual insights. Eihei Dogen, a prominent Japanese Zen Buddhist teacher, authored "Shobogenzo," a collection of his teachings which includes reflective writing and journal-style entries.

In Hinduism, the practice of keeping a spiritual diary is common among monks and devotees, such as the detailed diaries of Swami

Vivekananda which provide insight into his spiritual practices, travels, and the spread of Vedanta.

Contemporary Practice

In more recent times, notable figures like Thomas Merton continued the tradition of spiritual journaling. Merton, a 20th-century Trappist monk, wrote extensively about his spiritual journey, and his journals have inspired countless individuals seeking a deeper understanding of their faith.

In the modern era, spiritual journaling has been embraced by many different faiths and spiritual practices, continuing to serve as a tool for reflection, growth, and connection with the divine.

3

The Science of The Spiritual Practices: prayer, testimony, and gratitude

Scientists are renowned for meticulously documenting their work in journals. However, the practice of maintaining a spiritual journal can pose challenges for those with a practical scientific mindset. Nevertheless, gaining insight into the scientific principles underlying spiritual practices —such as prayer, thanksgiving, and testimony—can benefit scientifically inclined readers. Exploring scientific studies on the psychological and physiological effects of these practices reveals intriguing connections to brain health and overall well-being.

Prayer

Prayer is more than a spiritual exercise; it has tangible effects on our brain and body. Studies have shown that regular prayer can lead to decreased stress and anxiety levels. The act of prayer engages the same brain regions involved in attention and sensory awareness, fostering a state of calm and focus. Neuroscientific research using brain imaging techniques has demonstrated that individuals who engage in prayer or meditation exhibit increased activity in the prefrontal cortex, which is associated with higher-order brain functions such as self-regulation, problem-solving, and emotional control.

Testimony

Sharing personal testimonies, or narratives of spiritual experiences, also has profound benefits. This practice can enhance social connections and strengthen communities. On an individual level, recounting personal stories of faith can lead to greater self-awareness and personal growth. Psychologically, giving testimonies helps in processing life events, fostering an improved sense of meaning and purpose. Neurobiological studies suggest that storytelling activates the brain's reward circuits, releasing feel-good neurotransmitters like dopamine and oxytocin, which promote feelings of happiness and bonding.

Gratitude

Gratitude journaling has been widely studied, and the results are remarkable. Regularly noting things for which we are grateful can improve mood and increase overall life satisfaction. Gratitude practice has been shown to increase neural sensitivity in the medial prefrontal cortex, which is associated with learning and decision making. Physiologically, practicing gratitude can lower blood pressure, improve sleep quality, and boost immune function. Furthermore, gratitude helps in reducing symptoms of depression and anxiety by promoting a positive outlook on life, fostering resilience, and reducing negative emotions.

Forgiveness

While we do not go in depth into the topic of forgiveness in this book, a special note is included here because of its significant relationship to and impact on the practices of prayer and gratitude. Including the practice of forgiveness as part of your journaling routine can have profound psychological and physiological benefits. Delving into this spiritual practice through the lens of scientific study shows how powerful and transformative forgiving can be for overall well-being. In summary, forgiveness isn't just a spiritual concept—it has tangible effects on our minds and bodies. Consider incorporating forgiveness into your journaling practice for a healthier, more fulfilling life.

Spiritual Practice Meets Science

When we forgive, we release ourselves from emotional burdens. Scientifically, this correlates with reduced inflammation, improved immune function, and better overall well-being. Brain imaging studies demonstrate that forgiveness rewires neural pathways, leading to emotional balance and resilience.

Psychological Benefits

Forgiveness journaling helps in processing feelings of hurt, anger, and resentment, allowing individuals to move past negative emotions and fostering emotional healing. Writing about experiences that have caused pain, and subsequently reflecting on the choice to forgive, can lead to reduced symptoms of depression and anxiety. Studies have shown that individuals who regularly practice forgiveness report lower levels of stress and higher levels of life satisfaction and happiness. This practice equips individuals with tools for emotional regulation and resilience, aiding in personal development and emotional intelligence.

Physiological Benefits

The physiological benefits of forgiveness are equally significant. Forgiveness is associated with lower heart rate and blood pressure, which contribute to better cardiovascular health. It also reduces the levels of cortisol, a stress hormone, leading to overall stress reduction. Neuroscientific research indicates that when people forgive, there is increased activity in the prefrontal cortex, which is involved in complex cognitive behavior, personality expression, and decision making. There is also a reduction in amygdala activity, which is the part of the brain that processes fear and emotional responses, illustrating how forgiveness can lead to a calmer and more balanced emotional state.

Practical Tips for Forgiveness Journaling

Reflection: Start by reflecting on events or individuals that have caused pain or resentment. Write down your feelings honestly and without self-judgment.

Empathy: Try to view the situation from the other person's perspective. This can help in developing empathy and understanding.

Letting Go: Write a forgiveness letter, even if you do not send it. Express your intention to forgive and release the negative emotions tied to the event or person.

Gratitude: After expressing forgiveness, reflect on things for which you are grateful. This can help in shifting focus from negative emotions to positive ones.

Commitment to Forgiveness: Revisit your forgiveness journaling entries regularly to reaffirm your commitment to let go of resentment and embrace peace.

A personal example of the power of forgiveness.

Many years ago, I experienced the emotional pain of a broken heart that resulted from been betrayed by a close friend. During a prayerful moment, I felt compelled to extend forgiveness to the person who had hurt me. Remarkably, the act of forgiving brought immediate relief from the intense emotional distress I had been feeling. It allowed me to release the person from my heart and to let go of the toxic relationship and move forward in a healthier and more purposeful way.

Incorporating forgiveness into your journaling practice is not only about healing past wounds but also about nurturing a mindset of compassion and growth. Forgiveness plays a crucial role in the practice of journaling, especially when it comes to prayer and gratitude. Here are a few key points that highlight its importance:

1. **Emotional Healing:** Forgiveness allows you to release negative emotions, such as anger and resentment, which can be barriers to fully engaging in prayer and gratitude. Journaling about forgiveness helps you process and let go of these emotions.
2. **Spiritual Growth:** Forgiving others is often a core tenet in many spiritual traditions. Reflecting on forgiveness in your journal can deepen your spiritual journey and bring you closer to your faith.
3. **Enhanced Gratitude:** By forgiving others, you make space in your heart for gratitude. When you journal about forgiveness, you may find it easier to acknowledge and appreciate the positive aspects of your life.
4. **Personal Reflection:** Journaling about forgiveness creates an opportunity for introspection. This practice helps you understand your own reactions and behaviours, leading to personal growth and a more compassionate outlook on life.
5. **Prayer Focus:** Integrating forgiveness into your journaling can enhance your prayers. By addressing issues of forgiveness, you create a more open and sincere dialogue with your spirituality.

4

Real-Life Testimonials: The Transformative Power of Journaling

In this chapter, we will explore the profound and transformative impact that journaling can have on individuals' lives. Through sharing real-life testimonials, we aim to provide you with relatable experiences and motivation to continue or start your own journaling practice. These stories reflect personal growth, spiritual breakthroughs, and the deeply personal journey of connecting with one's inner self through the art of journaling.

Journaling can be a deeply personal and transformative practice, as illustrated by the experiences of many who have embraced it. Here is a collection of personal stories that highlight the powerful impact of journaling on individuals' lives. We thank the contributors for sharing their stories to encourage us.

My Personal Journey of Chronicling Dreams and Prophetic Insights

I started my journaling journey with a leather-bound journal, drawn to the classic, timeless feel of the cover. I felt as if I was chronicling history, with the sense that my writings might one day help me write a book or serve as examples to help others on their paths. Over the years, I have always kept a journal where I recorded my prayers, answers to prayers, gratitude, revelations and insights from scriptures or from sermons, dreams and prophetic insights. I often go back to see how many of these dreams and prophetic words have not only manifested but have transformed and changed my life for good. My journals became a repository of my dreams and insights, providing me with a way to track and reflect on the progression and fulfillment of these prophetic words. The practice of journaling not only offered me a therapeutic outlet but also served as a tool for spiritual growth and personal transformation. Recording my prayers, and what I hear from God in those moments has been a source of inspiration and guidance in my life, and many people have told me they emulated these practices from me over the years.

More recently, as I began my training into transformational coaching and sitting at the feet of and learning from great leaders like Mary Morrissey, Dean Graziosi, Myron Golden, and Tony Robbins, I realize that journaling is a critical part of the life of successful people. This has increased my appetite and motivation for journaling even more.

Testimonial 1: Emily's Journey to Self-Discovery

"Journaling became my sanctuary. Every morning I wrote down my prayers, my worries, and my dreams. As I filled pages with my thoughts, I began to uncover parts of myself I never knew existed."

Emily, a 32-year-old teacher, shares how journaling helped her navigate through a challenging period in her life. She recounts how writing prayers and reflections in her journal enabled her to discover her true passions and renewed her faith. Emily describes how this practice became a cornerstone in her daily routine, leading to significant personal growth and deeper spiritual connection.

Testimonial 2: Mark's Spiritual Breakthrough

"The act of writing down my gratitude every night brought a profound sense of peace into my life. It shifted my perspective, making me more aware of the blessings, both big and small, that I had been ignoring."

Mark, a 45-year-old entrepreneur, experienced a spiritual breakthrough through the simple act of journaling his gratitude. His testimonial highlights how focusing on gratitude transformed his outlook on life and improved his mental well-being. Mark shares specific instances where documenting his gratitude led to unexpected answered prayers and a stronger sense of purpose and joy.

Testimonial 3: Sarah's Healing Process

"Writing down my testimony freed me from the chains of my past. It was liberating to see my journey of healing and growth on paper. My journal became a testament to God's work in my life."

Sarah, a 29-year-old nurse, used journaling as a form of therapy to heal from past traumas. By documenting her testimonies, she found solace and strength. Sarah explains how revisiting her journal entries allowed her to recognize and celebrate her progress, deepening her faith and sense of self-worth. Her story emphasizes the therapeutic power of writing and reflection.

Testimonial 4: John's Path to Motivation and Discipline

"Maintaining a journaling practice taught me discipline and kept me motivated. Every goal I wrote down was a step towards achieving it. My journal was my accountability partner."

John, a 38-year-old fitness coach, shares how journaling helped him maintain motivation and discipline in his personal and professional life. His testimonial outlines how setting goals in his journal and tracking his progress kept him focused and committed. John provides practical tips on using journaling as a tool for accountability and personal development.

Testimonial 5: Lisa's Deepened Connection with Faith

"Through journaling, I found a new way to converse with God. My journal became a space for intimate and honest communication with the divine. It transformed my spiritual journey."

Lisa, a 50-year-old homemaker, describes how journaling deepened her spiritual connection and enriched her faith. Her story illustrates how integrating prayer into her journaling practice brought clarity, comfort, and a profound sense of divine presence in her daily life. Lisa's experience highlights journaling as a transformative spiritual tool.

These testimonials reflect the diverse ways in which journaling can bring about personal growth and spiritual breakthroughs. The courage and wisdom shared by Emily, Mark, Sarah, John, and Lisa serve as a source of inspiration for anyone looking to embark on or enhance their journaling journey. Remember, your journal is a private sanctuary where you can explore, heal, and grow. Let these stories motivate you to harness the power of journaling in your own life.

5

Journaling Prayer, Testimony, and Gratitude

Journaling can become a powerful tool that combines three essential aspects of spiritual growth: prayer, testimony, and thanksgiving. Starting a prayer, testimony, and gratitude journal is a beautiful way to deepen your connection with God. It is like having a personal conversation with Him on paper.

A prayer journal is a place where you record your conversations with God. It is a personal space to pour out your heart, express your thoughts, and communicate with the Divine. In your prayer journal, you can write down your prayers, petitions, and intercessions, as well as reflect on Scriptures that resonate with you, share your struggles, doubts, and joys with God, as well as express gratitude for answered prayers or unexpected blessings.

A testimony journal captures your personal stories of God's work in your life. It is a place to celebrate His faithfulness and share your experiences with others. In your testimony journal, you can write about answered prayers, miracles, and moments of divine intervention, document how God transformed your life, healed you, or guided your path, share stories of forgiveness, redemption, and spiritual growth, reflect on encounters with God's grace and love, and encourage others by sharing how God has been faithful in your personal journey.

A gratitude journal focuses on cultivating a thankful heart. It encourages you to recognize and appreciate the goodness in your life by shifting your perspective from what is lacking to recognizing God's abundant blessings. In your gratitude journal, you can list things you are thankful for each day, acknowledge both big and small blessings, reflect on moments of grace, kindness, and provision, express gratitude for relationships, health, opportunities, and simple pleasures, as well as shift your perspective from what is lacking to what's abundant.

Why Combine prayer, testimony, and thanksgiving?

- **Holistic Growth**: Integrating prayer, testimony, and gratitude fosters holistic spiritual growth. It aligns your heart with God's purposes.
- **Synergy:** When prayer and gratitude intersect, they create a powerful synergy. Praying with a grateful heart enhances your connection with God.
- **Mindset Shift:** Regularly expressing gratitude shifts your focus away from negativity and fosters contentment.
- **Intimacy with God:** As you converse with God in your journal, you deepen your relationship with Him.
- **Remembering God's Faithfulness:** Your testimony journal reminds you of God's past faithfulness, strengthening your faith for the present and future. Over time, your journal becomes a testimony of God's faithfulness, answered prayers, and blessings.
- **Gratitude as Worship:** Gratitude is a form of worship. When you express thankfulness, you honour God and recognize His hand in your life.

Reflection

Do you practice prayer, testimony, and thanksgiving? How could a journal help you be more intentional about these practices?

6
⁓

Journaling Your Prayers

"The reality is, my prayers don't change God. But, I am convinced prayer changes me. Praying boldly boots me out of that stale place of religious habit into authentic connection with God Himself."
Lysa TerKeurst

Prayer, according to the Bible, is **communication with God.** It is a two-way dialogue where we express our love, gratitude, and dependence on Him. Through prayer, we pour out our hearts and listen for God's guidance and wisdom. Prayer is essential for several reasons:

1. **Prayer Makes Us More Like Jesus:** If we look at the life of Jesus, we see that He prayed—with others, for others, and on His own. It was a fundamental part of how He approached each day and every decision. Prayer equipped Him for the battles He faced, kept alive the intimate relationship with His Father, and revealed God's desires and direction. As we pray, we become more like Jesus, and prayer changes us., Acts 2:42 - And they continued steadfastly in the apostles' doctrine and fellowship, and in breaking of bread, and in prayers.
2. **Growing Closer to God**: When we pray, we draw closer to

God. Spending time talking and listening to Him deepens our relationship. As we know Him more, fear diminishes, and courage prevails.' Psalms 145:18 - *The LORD is nigh unto all them that call upon him, to all that call upon him in truth.*

3. **Aligning with God's Will:** Prayer helps us surrender our lives to God, seeking His guidance. It aligns us with His purpose and plan for our lives.[xix]

4. **Acknowledging God's Control:** Prayer reminds us that God is in control. It shifts our focus from self-centeredness to concern for others. John 15:1-3 - *I am the true vine, and my Father is the husbandman.*

5. **Connection with the Divine:** Prayer is our lifeline to God. It is like picking up the phone and having a heart-to-heart conversation with our Heavenly Father. Through prayer, we express our joys, sorrows, fears, and hopes. It is a direct line to the One who loves us unconditionally. Ephesians 6:18 - *Praying always with all prayer and supplication in the Spirit, and watching thereunto with all perseverance and supplication for all saints.*

6. **Guidance and Wisdom:** When we seek God's guidance through prayer, we invite His wisdom into our decisions. Whether it is choosing a career path, navigating relationships, or facing challenges, prayer helps us discern the best course of action. The Bible encourages us to ask for wisdom, and God promises to provide it. Luke 11:2 - *And he said unto them, when ye pray, say, Our Father which art in heaven, Hallowed be thy name. Thy kingdom come. Thy will be done, as in heaven, so in earth.*

7. **Gratitude and Contentment:** Prayer cultivates gratitude. When we pause to thank God for His blessings—both big and small—we shift our focus from what we lack to what we have. Gratitude breeds contentment and joy. Colossians 4:2 - *Continue in prayer, and watch in the same with thanksgiving.*

8. **Strength in Trials:** Life can be tough. Prayer does not guarantee a trouble-free existence, but it equips us to face adversity with resilience. We find strength, courage, and peace as we lay our burdens

before God. James 5:13 - *Is any among you afflicted? let him pray. Is any merry? let him sing psalms.*

9. **Intercession for Others:** Prayer is not just about our needs; it is also about lifting others up. When we intercede for family, friends, and even strangers, we participate in God's work of healing, comfort, and transformation. Romans 1:9-10 - *For God is my witness, whom I serve with my spirit in the gospel of his Son, that without ceasing I make mention of you always in my prayers.*

10. **Spiritual Growth:** Consistent prayer deepens our faith. It is like watering a plant—it nourishes our spiritual roots. As we spend time with God, we become more attuned to His voice and grow in intimacy with Him. Luke 18:1 - *And he spake a parable unto them to this end, that men ought always to pray, and not to faint.*

11. **Prayer is communion with our Creator**—a loving fellowship that brings peace, guidance, and strength in life's challenges. Remember, prayer is not a ritual; it is a relationship. It is an ongoing conversation that shapes our hearts, minds, and lives.

Writing down your prayers

2And the LORD answered me, and said, Write the vision, and make it plain upon tables, that he may run that readeth it. 3For the vision is yet for an appointed time, but at the end it shall speak, and not lie: though it tarry, wait for it; because it will surely come, it will not tarry.
Habakkuk 2:2-3 (KJV)

Habakkuk 2:2-3 provides valuable insight into the practice of writing down prayers. Writing down prayers helps us articulate our thoughts and emotions more clearly. When we put our prayers on paper, we gain clarity about our desires, concerns, and hopes. Writing down the conversations with God helps to create a record of the conversation, so you do not forget what you said or what you asked during the period of waiting. Just as God instructed Habakkuk to write down the vision, our written prayers serve as reminders of God's promises and faithfulness. When we look back at our recorded prayers, we see how God has answered, guided, and sustained us over time.

Habakkuk 2:3 emphasizes waiting for the fulfillment of the vision. Writing down prayers encourages and builds patience and trust. We document our requests, knowing that God's timing is perfect—even if it seems delayed. Our written prayers become a testament to our faith in His promises.

There is clearly a strong spiritual benefit and precedence for keeping a prayer journal. Write down your heart's desires, praises, and petitions. It is a powerful way to deepen your relationship with God and witness His work in your life. Writing down your prayers offers several benefits that can enhance your spiritual journey and deepen your connection with God. Here are some reasons why you might consider writing down your prayers:

1. **Remembrance of God's Answers:** Often, we pray fervently, but once God answers our prayers, we may forget to acknowledge His provision. Writing down your prayers helps you track and remember when God responds to your requests.
2. **Inspiration in Prayer:** Unlike monotonous spoken prayers, writing them down adds an element of inspiration and excitement. Putting pen to paper intentionally engages your mind and heart more.
3. **Extended Time with God:** If you find it challenging to pray for extended periods, writing provides a way to spend more time in conversation with God. As you express your thoughts in writing, you engage in a deeper dialogue with Him.
4. **Relaxation and Calmness:** When you are feeling anxious, stressed, or depressed, writing out your prayers can be a soothing and calming practice. It allows you to convey your emotions and thoughts to God, easing negativity and promoting relaxation.
5. **Joy and Gratitude:** The act of writing often floods your mind with thoughts, leading to feelings of joy and gratitude. As you

express your needs, joys, and heartbreaks, you become more aware of God's presence and provision.

6. **Less Stale Prayer Life:** Writing down prayers prevents your prayer life from becoming monotonous. It adds variety and freshness, making your conversations with God more dynamic and meaningful.

7. **Praying Even When You Do Not Feel Like It:** There are times when we do not want to pray, but writing allows us to express our hearts even during those moments. It bridges the gap between our emotions and our commitment to seek God.

Habakkuk 2:2-3 (KJV) encourages: *"Write the vision, and make it plain upon tables, that he may run that readeth it."* Writing down your prayers creates a permanent record, helping you remember God's faithfulness and the promises you have made to pray for others. So, grab your pen and paper, or use digital tools, and start writing your heartfelt prayers today!

What to write in your prayer journal

A prayer journal is a beautiful way to record your spiritual journey, express your heart, and deepen your relationship with God. Here are some ideas for what you can write in your prayer journal:

1. **Gratitude:** Begin by expressing gratitude. Write down things you are thankful for—big or small. Acknowledge God's blessings, answered prayers, and the beauty around you.

2. **Praise and Worship:** Use your journal to praise God. Write to God about His awesomeness! Reflect on His character, love, majesty, and faithfulness. Write down verses, hymns, or songs that resonate with you. Praise Him for who He is.

3. **Confession:** Talk to God about your weaknesses and shortcomings. Be honest and transparent with God. Confess your sins, shortcomings, and areas where you need His forgiveness. Pour out

your heart, knowing that He is merciful. Confession allows for healing and forgiveness.

4. **Requests (Supplication):** Humbly ask God for what is on your heart. Share your needs and desires. Pray for yourself, family, friends, and the world. Be specific. Write down prayer requests and intercede for others.
5. **Personal Reflection:** Use your journal as a space for self-reflection. Write about your struggles, joys, fears, and hopes. Pour out your emotions.
6. **God's Promises:** Document promises from Scripture. When you encounter a promise, write it down and claim it in prayer.
7. **Silent Listening:** Sometimes, sit quietly and listen. Write down any impressions, thoughts, or nudges you feel from the Holy Spirit.
8. **Dreams and Visions:** If you have dreams or spiritual visions, jot them down. Seek God's interpretation and guidance.
9. **Reflection on Sermons or Devotions:** After reading a devotional or hearing a sermon, write down key takeaways and how they impacted you.
10. **Letters to God:** Imagine writing a letter to God. Pour out your heart, express your love, doubts, and longings. It is a personal conversation.
11. **Prayer for Others:** Dedicate pages to praying for specific people—family, friends, leaders, and those in need. Write their names and needs.
12. **Seasonal Reflections:** During holidays, seasons, or significant life events, reflect on their spiritual significance. Write prayers related to these moments.
13. **Creative Expressions:** Use your journal for creative expression. Draw, doodle, or include art that reflects your prayers.
14. **Scripture Reflection:** Sometimes, you might not have the words to say. That is okay! Choose a Bible verse or passage that speaks to you. Write it out, meditate on it, and explore its meaning. How does it apply to your life?

15. **Verses to Pray:** Choose specific verses to pray based on different situations: For example:

- When you are afraid.
- When your heart is broken.
- When you need more faith.
- When you are alone.
- When you need forgiveness.
- When you need hope.
- When you want to worship and thank God.

Answered Prayers: When God answers your prayers, celebrate! Write about a time when God answered your prayer. Record how He worked in your life. Share your story and let others in on the ways prayer impacts your life. It encourages faith and reminds you of His faithfulness.

Pray then like this: "Our Father in heaven, hallowed be your name. Your kingdom come, your will be done, on earth as it is in heaven. Give us this day our daily bread, and forgive us our debts, as we also have forgiven our debtors. And lead us not into temptation but deliver us from evil. - Matthew 6:9-13 (ESV)

Remember, there is no right or wrong way to keep a prayer journal. It is a sacred space where you can be authentic with God. Let your heart flow onto the pages, and may your journal become a treasure of faith and intimacy.

Reflection

What did you learn from this chapter?

What issues and which people would you like to pray for?

7

Journaling Your Gratitude

Our inner thought patterns and behaviours don't always align seamlessly with the life we aspire to lead. Sometimes, we find ourselves fixated on scarcity and limitations, even as we yearn for abundance. Perhaps we harbour feelings of resentment when we long for more love, or maybe our actions—whether mental, emotional, or physical—are not in alignment with the ideal life we desire to live.

Our thought patterns, behaviours, and emotions collectively shape the energetic frequency of our existence. Having a sense of gratitude enables our energetic frequency to bring a new kind of harmony into our lives. Embracing gratitude can be transformative—it shifts our perspective and invites more positivity into our lives. Gratitude operates on a frequency of flow and expansion, harmonizing beautifully with abundance. When we cultivate gratitude, when we choose to be grateful instead of resentful and unappreciative, we open ourselves to deserving more—a key ingredient in creating a life in harmony, fuelled by our deepest desires.

The practice of gratitude journaling is the habit of recording and reflecting on things that you are grateful for on a regular basis. It is a popular practice in the field of positive psychology and is also referred to as "counting one's blessings" or "three good things."

Incorporating gratitude journaling into our daily routine is a powerful way to enhance our well-being. Whether we write in a physical journal or use digital tools, the act of acknowledging what we are thankful for brings positive changes to our lives. Even the little things we appreciate can transform our days into moments of thanksgiving and blessings.

Gratitude is a wonderful feeling. Identifying all that's good in our lives and giving thanks for it has a way of grounding us, reminding us that, no matter what, we are blessed to be on this planet every day. Counting our blessings helps to put frustrations and the bigger stressors in life into perspective. When we approach life from a vantage point of thankfulness, we are better able to see the upside or positives, even in the most difficult circumstances.

In his letter to the Thessalonian church, Paul reiterates the importance of gratitude: *"Give thanks in all circumstances; for this is the will of God in Christ Jesus for you."* 1 Thessalonians 5:18. Here, he reminds us that even in challenging situations, expressing gratitude aligns with God's purpose for our lives. In other words, God desires for us to always have a grateful outlook, regardless of the circumstances we find ourselves in. the power of gratitude or thankfulness can transform situations.

The Power of Gratitude Journaling

One way to hold on to the positive feelings or the good vibes of gratitude even longer, is to write it on paper.

This is the motivation behind the practice of gratitude journaling. It only takes a few minutes a day, but it can give you a lasting mood boost that can take you from feeling "okay" to feeling "great" on a more regular basis.

There are various benefits to gratitude journaling and several scientific studies provide evidence supporting its positive impact on our well-being.

Gratitude journaling involves regularly writing down things for which we are thankful. It is a simple practice that can have profound effects on our mental, emotional, and physical health. Here is how it works:

1. **Increased Happiness and Positive Emotions:**
    - When we express gratitude by jotting down what we appreciate, we activate positive emotions. It is like training our brain to notice the good in our lives.
    - Studies have shown that people who maintain gratitude journals tend to feel happier and experience fewer feelings of loneliness and isolation.
2. **Better Sleep Quality:**
    - Gratitude journaling before bedtime can lead to improved sleep. By focusing on positive aspects, we reduce anxiety and promote relaxation.
    - Quality sleep is essential for overall well-being, and gratitude plays a role in achieving it.
3. **Reduced Symptoms of Illness:**
    - Keeping a gratitude journal has been linked to better health outcomes. It is associated with lower stress levels, which in turn positively impacts our physical health,,,
    - By acknowledging the good, we may strengthen our immune system and reduce inflammation in the body.
4. **Enhanced Coping with Adversity:**
    - Gratitude helps us build resilience. When faced with challenges, recognizing the positive aspects—even small ones—can help us cope better. It does not negate the difficulties but provides a perspective that fosters emotional strength.
5. **Increased Happiness Among Adults and Children:**
    - Gratitude is not limited to age. Both adults and children benefit from gratitude practices. Children who engage in gratitude activities tend to experience more positive emotions and develop a sense of appreciation.
6. **Positive Impact on Mental Health:**
    - Gratitude journaling contributes to overall mental well-being. It encourages a shift from scarcity thinking to abundance. By focusing on what we are thankful for, we create a positive feedback loop in our minds.

The Science of Gratitude

Gratitude is not just a pleasant feeling; it has a neuroscientific basis. Research has shown that gratitude affects the brain:

- **Joy, Gratitude, and the Brain:** When we express gratitude and receive it in return, our brain releases dopamine and serotonin—two crucial neurotransmitters responsible for our emotions. These neurotransmitters create a sense of pleasure and contentment, leading to long-lasting happiness.
- **Gratitude and Relationships:** "Strong social connections play a crucial role in mental well-being, particularly for individuals who may already feel isolated due to poor mental health or substance use. A 2010 study explored the effects of gratitude on social relationships and found that expressing gratitude not only enhanced existing connections but also facilitated the creation of new ones. These healthy social interactions, in turn, contribute to improved mental health and overall positive health outcomes.
- **Anxiety and Gratitude:**
    - A 2015 study using functional magnetic resonance imaging (fMRI) scans observed brain activity in individuals practicing gratitude. The findings revealed heightened activity in the prefrontal cortex, a region associated with decision-making, emotions, and social behaviour. Essentially, gratitude activates the prefrontal cortex, which helps regulate emotions, improve decision making and reduces anxiety. By practicing gratitude, we create a buffer against stress and worry., People who practiced writing gratitude letters were found to be grateful and more likely to continue to practice gratitude in the long term.
- **Gratitude and Grief:**
    - Even during challenging times, finding moments of gratitude can ease grief and emotional pain.
    - It does not diminish the loss but provides solace.
- **Resilience and Gratitude:**

- Grateful individuals tend to bounce back from adversity more effectively. The brain's plasticity allows us to rewire our responses through gratitude.
- **Depression and Gratitude:**
  - Gratitude interventions have been used as part of depression treatment. Focusing on positive aspects can counter depressive thoughts.[7]

Reward System Activation: At its core, gratitude stimulates the brain's reward system, a complex network of neural circuits responsible for processing pleasurable experiences and reinforcing behaviours. When we experience gratitude, our brain releases a cascade of neurotransmitters, including dopamine and serotonin, often referred to as the brain's "feel-good" chemicals because of their association with feelings of pleasure and contentment.

Robert Emmons, a professor at the University of California, Davis, specializes in the study of gratitude and has conducted extensive research on its impact. He emphasises the transformative power of gratitude and how it shapes our perception of life and our interactions with others. Emmons says: *"When I see life as full of gifts and I'm a receiver—our entire life is one big gift—it enables me to organize my experience. Seeing myself as the recipient of giftedness as well as a potential giver of my own gifts onto other people—that constitutes my identity: a recipient as well as a giver of grace."*

Here are various research-based tips from Emmons, for reaping the greatest psychological rewards from your gratitude journal.

Do not just go through the motions. Research by psychologist Sonja Lyubomirsky and others suggests that journaling is more effective if you first make the conscious decision to become happier and more grateful. *"Motivation to become happier plays a role in the efficacy of journaling,"* says Emmons.

Go for depth over breadth. Elaborating in detail about a particular thing for which you are grateful carries more benefits than a superficial list of many things.

Get personal. Focusing on *people* to whom you are grateful has more of an impact than focusing on *things* for which you are grateful.

Try subtraction, not just addition. One effective way of stimulating gratitude is to reflect on what your life would be like *without* certain blessings, rather than just tallying up all those good things.

Savor surprises. Try to record events that were unexpected or surprising, as these tend to elicit stronger levels of gratitude.

Do not overdo it. Writing occasionally (once or twice per week) is more beneficial than daily journaling. In fact, one study by Lyubomirsky and her colleagues found that people who wrote in their gratitude journals once a week for six weeks reported boosts in happiness afterward; people who wrote three times per week did not. *"We adapt to positive events quickly, especially if we constantly focus on them,"* says Emmons. *"It seems counterintuitive, but it is how the mind works."*

Your gratitude journal is a personal endeavour that must be unique to you and your life. Remember, even the little things we appreciate can transform our days into moments of thanksgiving and blessings.

Thanksgiving prayer examples

Here are some **beautiful Thanksgiving prayers** to inspire gratitude and express thanks to God:

- **Traditional Prayer for Thanksgiving**:
  "Bless us, oh Lord, and these Thy gifts which we are about to receive from Thy bounty through Christ our Lord. Amen."
- **Psalm of Thanksgiving** (based on Psalm 103:1-6):
  "Bless the LORD, O my soul, and all that is within me, bless his holy name! Forget not all his benefits: forgiveness of iniquity, healing of diseases, redemption from the pit, steadfast love, and mercy.

May our youth be renewed like the eagle's. The LORD works righteousness and justice for all who are oppressed."
- **Thanksgiving Prayer from the Bible** (1 Thessalonians 5:18):[12]
"Give thanks in all circumstances; for this is God's will for you in Christ Jesus."

Heavenly Father, As we gather on this day of Thanksgiving, we remember the words of Holy Scripture that call us to give thanks in all circumstances. Lord, we thank You for the countless blessings You have bestowed upon us, both in times of joy and in times of challenge. We are grateful for the love of family and friends who surround us, for the food on our table, and for the shelter over our heads. ◈

- **Simple Christian Thanksgiving Prayer:**
"Thank you, Lord, for bringing us all together today. Though this one day every year we come to you in gratitude, we are grateful year-round for what you have provided for us."
- **Prayer of Thanksgiving:**
"God of all blessings, source of all life, giver, we thank you for the gift of life: for the breath that sustains life, for the food of this earth that nurtures life, for the love of family and friends without which there would be no life."
- **Prayer of Gratitude to Jesus Christ:**

"Jesus Christ, my Lord and God, I give thanks for your loving-kindness and all the blessings You have richly bestowed upon me. I fall down in worship and adoration before You, the King of Glory."

- **Thank You, Lord!**
  - "Thank you, Lord, for all the blessings in my life. Thank you for the sun that rises each morning and the stars that shine each night. Thank you for the joy of friendship and the comfort of family. Thank you for the beauty of nature and

the mysteries of the universe. Thank you for your guidance and protection."
- Dear Lord, thank you for this meal and for all our many blessings. Amen.
- For flowers that bloom about our feet, Father, we thank Thee. For tender grass so fresh, so sweet, Father, we thank Thee. For the song of bird and hum of bee, for all things fair we hear or see, Father in heaven, we thank Thee. Amen.
- Thank you, Lord, for bringing us all together today. Though this one day every year we come to you in gratitude, we are grateful year-round for what you have provided for us. Amen. May these prayers inspire your heart with gratitude and deepen your connection with God.

"I will give to the Lord the thanks due to his righteousness, and I will sing praise to the name of the Lord, the Most High." - Psalm 7:17

Reflection
Is there anything for which you are thankful?

Has anyone done anything for you, or done some good that you could thank? Express your thanks or gratitude to them with a note or text message. List the names here, then send then a note to say thank you!

The Practice of Journaling Prayer, Testimony, and Gratitude

8

Journaling Your Testimony

Definition of Testimony: Testimony involves being a witness, proclaiming God's truth. It is a declaration of faith, sharing personal experiences of God's presence and work in our lives. In Scripture, testimony relies on objective facts and historical reliability.

Testimony, according to the Bible, holds profound significance. Let us explore some biblical references to testimony:

- Jesus emphasizes the validity of two witnesses for truth: **John 8:17-18**: *"It is also written in your law, that the testimony of two men is true."*
- Triumph over evil through the blood of the Lamb and the word of testimony. **Revelation 12:11**: *"They triumphed over him by the blood of the Lamb and by the word of their testimony; they did not love their lives so much as to shrink from death."*
- Do not be ashamed of testifying about the Lord. **2 Timothy 1:8**: *"So do not be ashamed of the testimony about our Lord or of me his prisoner. Rather, join with me in suffering for the gospel, by the power of God."*
- Believing in God's testimony brings life, even eternal life. **1 John 5:10-11**: *"Whoever believes in the Son of God accepts this testimony.*

Whoever does not believe God has made him out to be a liar, because they have not believed the testimony God has given about his Son. And this is the testimony: God has given us eternal life, and this life is in his Son."

- Martyrs maintain their testimony even in death. **Revelation 6:9**: *"When he opened the fifth seal, I saw under the altar the souls of those who had been slain because of the word of God and the testimony they had maintained."*
- The gospel as a testimony to all nations. **Matthew 24:14**: *"And this gospel of the kingdom will be preached in the whole world as a testimony to all nations, and then the end will come."*
- Jesus testifies to God's Word. **Revelation 1:2**: *"...who testifies to everything he saw—that is, the word of God and the testimony of Jesus Christ."*
- Samaritans believed due to the woman's testimony. **John 4:39**: Many of the Samaritans from that town believed in him because of the woman's testimony, *"He told me everything I ever did."*
- Jesus' testimony and the Father's witness. **John 5:32-33**: *"There is another who testifies in my favour, and I know that his testimony about me is true. You have sent to John, and he has testified to the truth."*

In essence, our testimony reflects God's work in our lives—a powerful tool for justice, truth, evangelism and faith-building.

Why Testifying Matters

Testifying to God's goodness holds immense significance in our spiritual journey. When God does something miraculous in our lives, it is not merely for our benefit but also for His glory.

Testifying matters for several reasons, especially in the context of faith and personal experiences. Here is why testifying matters:

1. **Glorifying God**: Our testimonies magnify God's power and

faithfulness. By sharing what He has done, we honour Him and acknowledge His sovereignty. As Revelation 12:11 says, "They triumphed over him by the blood of the Lamb and by the word of their testimony."
2. **Defeating the Enemy**: When we testify, we weaken the enemy's hold on our lives. Our stories of God's goodness become weapons against darkness. The devil fears the impact of our testimonies.
3. **Biblical Foundation**: The Bible emphasizes testifying. Jesus Himself bore witness to the truth (John 2:25). The apostle Paul testified about the grace of God (Acts 20:24). Our testimonies align with this biblical pattern.
4. **Encouragement**: When we share our testimonies, we encourage others. Our stories of God's faithfulness, healing, or transformation inspire those facing similar challenges.
5. **Authenticity**: Testimonies reveal our authentic journey with God. They show vulnerability, struggles, and victories. Authenticity fosters genuine connections.
6. **Evangelism**: Testimonies are powerful evangelistic tools. Nonbelievers often relate to personal stories more than theological arguments.
7. **Remembrance**: Testimonies remind us of God's goodness. When life gets tough, recalling how God worked in the past strengthens our faith.
8. **Unity**: Shared testimonies unite believers. We celebrate God's work together, reinforcing our sense of community.

Remember the leper who approached Jesus in Matthew 8:1-4? His straightforward plea reflects our desperation when facing life's challenges. We seek help, grasp for hope, and trust in God's power. So, when God has come through for us, we should testify. It honours Him and encourages and emboldens us. Go ahead and testify boldly! Share how God has intervened in your life. Whether it is healing, provision, or deliverance, your story matters. By doing so, you contribute to God's kingdom and inspire others to trust Him.

Documenting Testimonies of Answered Prayers.

Documenting testimonies of answered prayers serves several important purposes in our spiritual journey. Let us explore some reasons why this is valuable:

Strengthening Faith: When we write down how God has answered our prayers, it **strengthens our faith**. Seeing tangible evidence of His faithfulness reminds us that He is actively involved in our lives.

Encouragement: Documenting answered prayers provides **encouragement**. During challenging times, reviewing past testimonies reminds us that God is dependable and trustworthy. It encourages us to keep praying and seeking Him.

Gratitude: Writing down answered prayers allows us to **express gratitude**. Gratefulness is a powerful spiritual practice. When we acknowledge God's provision, our hearts overflow with thanksgiving.

Remembrance: Our memories can be fleeting. Documenting answered prayers helps us **remember** specific instances when God intervened. It is easy to forget His goodness, but written records keep those memories alive.

Inspiration for Others: Sharing our testimonies can inspire others. When we document how God worked in our lives, it becomes a **witness** to His power. Others may find hope and encouragement through our stories.

Faith Legacy: Imagine passing down your prayer journals to future generations. Your documented testimonies become part of your faith legacy, inspiring you to trust God.[xxxix]

> *"And they overcame him by the blood of the Lamb, and by the word of their testimony; and they loved not their lives unto the death."*
> **Revelation 12:11**

So, whether you use a journal, a digital note, or even a simple clipboard, consider documenting your answered prayers. It is a beautiful way to honour God and celebrate His work in your life.

Reflection
What amazing thing did God do?
_____
_____
_____
_____
_____

How did you see divine intervention at work in your personal life? Family? Business? Career? Finances? Other areas?
_____
_____
_____
_____
_____
_____
_____
_____
_____
_____
_____
_____
_____

9

Maintaining Motivation for Your Journal

Maintaining motivation for your journal is essential for a consistent and meaningful practice. Regular practice reinforces positive habits. Staying motivated ensures that we consistently engage in these spiritual practices, making them an integral part of our lives. Life's challenges can dampen our enthusiasm. Motivation keeps us resilient, allowing us to turn to prayer, gratitude, and testimony even during difficult times. These practices provide emotional support and perspective. Motivation encourages us to be mindful. When we intentionally journal prayers, gratitude, and testimonies, we become more aware of God's presence and blessings. Mindfulness enhances our spiritual experience.

Staying Inspired on the journey

Consistency deepens our connection with God and helps us grow spiritually. Here are some practical tips to help you stay inspired:

1. **Aesthetics:** You have purchased a **journal you love** -an aesthetically pleasing journal. This will encourage you to feel more excited

to write. Use coloured pens, highlighters, and sticky notes to add visual appeal.

2. **Create a Sacred Space**: Find a quiet spot where you can **enjoy writing**. Free yourself from distractions like to-do lists or chores. Whether it is a cozy corner, a sunlit room, or a peaceful garden, make it a place where you can connect with God.
3. **Set Realistic Goals**: Instead of pressuring yourself to write every day, set **achievable goals**. Maybe you will write weekly or whenever you can. God appreciates your effort, even if it is not daily. Give yourself grace.
4. **Use Prompts**: If you ever draw a blank, use prompts to kickstart you are writing. Here are a few ideas:

    - **Gratitude**: List things for which you are thankful.
    - **Confession**: Talk to God about your weaknesses and shortcomings.
    - **Praise**: Write about how awesome God is.

1. **Track Your Prayers**: Consider tracking your prayers over time. You can:
2. **Record Requests**: Write down specific prayer requests.

    - **Celebrate Answers**: When God answers, celebrate and document it.
    - **Reflect on Growth**: Observe how your prayers evolve and how God works in your life.

1. **Be Authentic**: When you sit down to write, **be real**. Pour out your thoughts, feelings, and desires. Do not hold back. God wants to hear your heart.
2. **Include Scripture**: Copy down verses or quotes that resonate with you. Let God's Word inspire and encourage you. These references will uplift you during challenging times.
3. **Stay Consistent**: Consistency matters more than frequency.

Whether it is daily, weekly, or occasional, **show up**. God honours your commitment.

Reflection and Review Techniques

Reviewing and reflecting on past journal entries is essential to unlocking the full potential of your journaling practice. By revisiting your writings, you can identify patterns, track progress, and gain valuable insights about yourself. Here are some effective techniques to help you reflect and review your journal entries:

Methods for Reflection and Review
Identifying Patterns

Theme Analysis: Read through your entries to identify recurring themes or subjects. This can help you understand persistent thoughts or concerns.

Highlighting Key Points: Use colored markers or digital highlights to note significant emotions, events, or lessons. This visually distinguishes notable entries for easier reference.

Tracking Progress

Monthly Reviews: Set aside time at the end of each month to read and reflect on your entries. Note any achievements, setbacks, or significant changes.

Annual Reviews: Perform a comprehensive review of your journal entries at the end of the year. Summarize key insights, achievements, and lessons learned.

Gaining Insights

Themed Reflections: Select a theme (e.g., career, relationships, personal growth) and review only the entries related to that theme. This focused approach can provide deeper insights into specific areas of your life.

Questions for Reflection: Use reflective questions to guide your review, such as:

- What patterns do I notice in my thoughts or behaviors?
- How have I grown or changed over the past [month/year]?
- What recurring challenges do I face, and how can I address them?

Example Practices

Highlight Achievements and Challenges: At regular intervals, reflect on your entries to celebrate achievements and address challenges.

Create Summary Pages: Dedicate a page at the end of each month to summarize your reflections, highlighting key takeaways and goals for the next month.

By incorporating these techniques into your journaling routine, you can gain a deeper understanding of yourself, track your progress, and make informed decisions for your future.

Remember, your prayer journal is a personal journey—a conversation between you and God. Let it be a source of joy, reflection, and growth.

The **length of each entry** in your prayer journal is entirely up to you! There is no strict rule or requirement. However, here are some considerations:

1. **Quality Over Quantity**: Focus on the **quality** of your entries rather than their length. A heartfelt, concise prayer can be more powerful than a lengthy one filled with empty words.
2. **Be Authentic**: Write until you have expressed what is on your heart. It could be a few sentences or several paragraphs. Authenticity matters more than length.
3. **Time Commitment**: Consider the **time** you have available. If you are busy, a shorter entry is perfectly fine. If you have more time, feel free to write more.

4. **Reflect and Meditate**: Sometimes, a brief entry allows you to **reflect and meditate** on specific aspects of your prayer. Other times, you might want to explore a topic in depth.
5. **Variety**: Mix it up! Some days, write a longer entry with detailed requests. On other days, jot down a quick thanksgiving or a single verse that touched your heart.

Again, your prayer journal is a personal space. Let it flow naturally, and let God guide your words.

The frequency of writing in your journal

The frequency of writing in your prayer journal **is a** personal choice, and there's no one-size-fits-all answer. However, here are some considerations to help you decide:

1. **Daily**: Many people find daily journaling beneficial. It establishes a consistent habit and keeps your spiritual life at the forefront. Consider writing in your prayer journal every morning or evening.
2. **Weekly**: If daily feels overwhelming, aim for weekly entries. Choose a specific day each week to reflect, pray, and record your thoughts.
3. **As Needed**: Write whenever you feel prompted by the Holy Spirit or when you encounter significant moments—both joyful and challenging. Let your heart guide you.
4. **During Special Seasons**: During seasons like Lent, Advent, or other spiritual observances, commit to more frequent journaling. It can deepen your experience.
5. **After Significant Events**: After attending a retreat, hearing a powerful sermon, or experiencing a life event, write about it. Capture the spiritual impact.
6. **When Seeking Guidance**: If you are seeking direction or clarity, write down your prayers and listen for God's response.
7. **Before Bed**: Some people find nighttime conducive for reflection.

Writing before bed allows you to process the day and surrender it to God.

Remember, consistency matters more than frequency. Whether it is daily, weekly, or occasional, the key is to **be intentional**. Your prayer journal is a sacred space—a conversation between you and God. Let it flow naturally, and let the Spirit guide your pen.

Missing a day of writing in your prayer journal is perfectly normal and happens to everyone. Here are some steps you can take when you miss a day:

1. **Do not Worry**: First, **do not stress** about it. Life gets busy, and sometimes we forget. God understands.
2. **Extend Grace to Yourself**: Remember that **grace** is essential. God does not keep score. He loves you regardless of how often you write.
3. **Reflect on Why**: Take a moment to **reflect on why** you missed a day. Was it busyness, forgetfulness, or lack of motivation? Understanding the reason can help you adjust.
4. **Catch Up**: If you missed a day, consider **catching up**. Write a brief entry about the missed day, even if it is a summary. It is not about perfection; it is about consistency.
5. **Start Fresh**: Each day is a new opportunity. **Start fresh**. Write today's prayers and let go of any guilt about the missed day.
6. **Set Reminders**: Use reminders on your phone or sticky notes to prompt you to write. Consistency often comes with intentional reminders.
7. **Learn from It**: Use the missed day as a **learning experience**. What can you do differently to stay consistent?

In summary, your journal helps you to draw closer to God. Whether you write daily or occasionally, what matters most is your heart's posture—a desire to connect with Him.

Overcoming writer's block.

When you find yourself unsure of what to write in your prayer journal, do not worry! It is normal to experience moments of uncertainty. Here are some helpful steps to overcome writer's block and keep your journaling practice meaningful:

1. **Start with Gratitude**: Begin by expressing gratitude. Write down three things you are thankful for today. It could be as simple as a sunny morning, a kind word from a friend, or a warm cup of tea.
2. **Reflect on Your Day**: Consider the events, emotions, and experiences you have encountered. Reflect on how God has been present in your day. Write about any challenges, joys, or surprises.
3. **Read Scripture**: Open your Bible to a random page or choose a favourite verse. Write it down and reflect on its meaning. How does it apply to your life right now?
4. **Pray for Others**: Dedicate a section of your journal to praying for others. Write down the names of family members, friends, colleagues, or anyone in need. Intercede on their behalf.
5. **Write a Letter to God**: Imagine you are writing a letter to God. Pour out your heart. Share your hopes, fears, dreams, and questions. Be honest and vulnerable.
6. **Describe Your Surroundings**: Look around you. Describe the room, the view outside, or the sounds you hear. Sometimes, observing the present moment sparks inspiration.
7. **Ask God for Guidance**: Pray for clarity and inspiration. Ask God to guide your thoughts and words. Trust that He will lead you.
8. **Use Prompts**: If you still feel stuck, use prompts like:
    - "Lord, teach me…"
    - "Lord, lead me…"
    - "Lord, show me…"
    - "Help me understand…"
    - "Help me to see or discern…"
    - "I'm struggling with…"
    - "Thank you for…"

- "I am grateful and thankful for…"
- "Show me your will in…"
- "Open my eyes to see…"

9. **Write a Poem or Song**: Get creative! Write a short poem or a few lines of a song. Express your feelings through art.
10. **Draw or Doodle**: If words fail, draw or doodle. Let your creativity flow. Sometimes visual expressions can convey what words cannot.

Remember, there is no right or wrong way to write in your journal. It is a conversation between you and God. Be patient with yourself and allow the Holy Spirit to guide your pen.

Dealing with Unanswered Prayers

"So, what if my prayers are not answered?"

When it seems like your prayers are **unanswered**, it can be discouraging. Here are some **helpful steps** to consider:

1. **Check Your Life**: Reflect on your life. Are there any **unresolved issues**, unconfessed sins, or areas where you need to make amends? Sometimes, our spiritual condition affects our prayers.
2. **Pray Rightfully**: Evaluate your prayer approach. Are you praying **according to God's will**? Seek His guidance and align your requests with His purposes. Remember, God's timing and ways are higher than ours.[xliii]
3. **Check Your Faith**: Examine your faith. Doubt can hinder answered prayers. Jesus said, "According to your faith, let it be done to you" (Matthew 9:29). Trust that God hears you and is working, even if you do not see immediate results.[xliii]
4. **Seek Community**: Surround yourself with **encouraging people** who can pray for you. Connect with others who have faced similar struggles. Sharing burdens lightens the load and strengthens your faith.[xliii]
5. **Remember God's Character**: Remind yourself of God's attributes

—His love, wisdom, and faithfulness. Even when answers delay, trust that He is still good and knows what is best for you.[xliii]

6. **Persist in Prayer**: Jesus taught persistence in prayer (Luke 18:1-8). Keep seeking, knocking, and asking. God honours perseverance. Your breakthrough may be closer than you think.[xliii]
7. **Seek His Will**: Sometimes, God's answer is a **"no"** or **"not now."** Trust that His plan is better than ours. Seek His will above our desires. Surrender to His wisdom and timing.[xliii]

Remember, God's ways are mysterious, and His timing is perfect. Keep seeking Him, even when answers seem elusive.

Staying faithful through the waiting

Staying motivated when your prayers seem unanswered **can** be challenging, but there are valuable perspectives to consider during these times:

1. **Remember God's Care and Love:** The enemy may try to convince you that God does not care about your needs or prayers. However, God knows your needs even before you ask (Matthew 6:8). Scriptures assure us that God cares for us: *"Cast your anxiety on Him, for He cares for you"* (1 Peter 5:7).
2. **Assurance of God's Listening Ear:** God hears every prayer, **even when it feels like** He has not answered. His eyes are on the righteous, and His ears are attentive to their cries (Psalm 34:15). The Holy Spirit intercedes for us, even when we do not know how to express our hearts (Romans 8:26).
3. **Understanding God's Responses:** Sometimes God's answer is a clear "yes," but other times it may be "no" or different from what we prayed for. God sees the bigger picture of our lives. He knows what is best for us, even if it does not align with our immediate desires.
4. **Eternal Perspective:** God's plans for us are good, and He promises

hope and a future (Jeremiah 29:11). Trust that God's timing and purposes extend beyond our present circumstances.

Persistent prayer is not about reminding God; it is about reminding ourselves that He is the source of our answers and needs. Even when it seems like our prayers go unanswered, God is at work in ways we may not fully understand.

Reflection

Reflect on this chapter. What are some key points you want to take note of?

_____
_____
_____
_____
_____
_____
_____

How will you use this information to support your approach to prayer practice?

_____
_____
_____
_____
_____
_____
_____

The Practice of Journaling Prayer, Testimony, and Gratitude - 67

10

Exploring Various Formats of Journaling

Journaling has evolved beyond the traditional pen-and-paper method, offering diverse formats that cater to different preferences and lifestyles. Each format provides unique benefits and can be seamlessly integrated into your daily routine. Let's delve into a few examples including digital journaling, visual journaling, and audio journaling to understand how each can enhance your journaling experience.

Digital Journaling
Benefits:
Convenience: Digital journals can be accessed anytime, anywhere, from your smartphone, tablet, or laptop.
Organization: Features like tagging, searching, and categorizing entries make it easier to locate past thoughts and ideas.
Multimedia Integration: Incorporate photos, videos, and links to enrich your entries.
Examples:
Morning Pages: Use a digital app like Notion or Evernote to write three pages of stream-of-consciousness thoughts each morning.

Daily Reflection: At the end of the day, capture highlights and lessons learned in a dedicated journal app.

Visual Journaling
Benefits:

Creative Expression: Combines art and writing, allowing for a more holistic expression of thoughts and emotions.

Mindfulness: The process of drawing or creating collages can be meditative and stress-reducing.

Memorable Entries: Visual elements can make entries more memorable and impactful.

Examples:

Artistic Diaries: Use sketchbooks to create daily or weekly entries that incorporate doodles, sketches, and mixed media art.

Bullet Journals: Organize your life with a bullet journal, using symbols, color codes, and illustrations to track tasks, habits, and goals.

Audio Journaling
Benefits:

Verbal Expression: Great for those who express themselves better verbally than in writing.

Convenience: Record entries on the go without needing a quiet or private space to write.

Emotion Tracking: Voice recordings capture the nuances of tone and inflection, providing deeper insight into your emotional state.

Examples:

Voice Memos: Use an app like Voice Memos or Otter to record daily reflections, dreams, or ideas as they come to you.

Prompt-Based Entries: Respond to journaling prompts verbally, creating a more dynamic and spontaneous journaling session.

Integration into Daily Routine

Here's how you can integrate these journaling formats into your routine:

- **Set Specific Times:** Dedicate a regular time each day for journaling. Combine different formats based on your schedule and needs.
- **Combine Formats:** Use a mix of digital, visual, and audio journaling to keep things interesting and cater to different aspects of your creativity and reflection.
- **Leverage Technology:** Utilize apps and tools that sync across devices, making it easier to maintain consistency and access your journal anytime.

By exploring these varied journaling formats, you can identify the one (or combination) that best suits your lifestyle and preferences, thereby enhancing your practice and reaping the full benefits of journaling.

Reflection

What type of journal appeals to you? Will you try a new journal format after reading this? Why?

11

Making Your Own Journal

How to make a journal

You do not need to feel left out if you cannot afford to purchase a sophisticated or expensive journal. You can DIY – do it yourself. You can purchase a plain journal or a blank notebook and convert that into your journal.

All you need is a good pen, and the optional ruler or some stickers and highlighter pens from the local stationary store to jazz up your journal, to your taste and style. You can check online for DIY Home made journal ideas.

In her Blog Post: **The Ultimate Guide to Prayer Journaling for Beginners**, LaToya Edwards provide some great tips on making your own prayer journal. I have incorporated some of their ideas here, that can be applied for a homemade (DIY journal).

Organising your journal

When setting up your journal, consider dedicating specific days to different aspects of your Theme. For instance, if you are making a prayer journal, choose a focus for each day. This could a focus on reflection for what has happened over the weekend, and praying based on your insights, revelations, or questions. Tuesday could be devoted to praying for your family's well-being, and reserve Wednesdays for praying for your friends. While some matters may require daily attention, spreading out the rest throughout the week can be beneficial.

While you will be spending less time in prayer each day, you will actually pray for far more things. Having a plan in place will help you remember, reduce overwhelm, and boost consistency. As you pray, you will gain confidence and overcome obstacles.

Your journal sections

There are many different sections that you can include inside your journal or notebook. Here are some mindfulness journal prompts related to prayer, gratitude, and goals that you can use for each day from Monday to Friday:

- **Monday (Vision or Goals)**: Set a specific goal for the day or week. Break down the steps needed to achieve it. Reflect on progress made toward your goals.
- **Tuesday (Prayer)**: Reflect on a specific prayer or intention for the week. Write about any spiritual insights or moments of connection. Consider how prayer impacts your mindset and well-being.
- **Wednesday (Gratitude)**: List three things you are grateful for today. Describe a moment that brought you joy or appreciation. Express gratitude for the people, experiences, or blessings in your life.
- **Thursday (Prayer)**: Write a heartfelt prayer or meditation. Explore any challenges or doubts related to your faith. Consider how prayer supports your emotional resilience.
- **Friday (Gratitude)**: Reflect on the week's highlights and positive moments. Identify what has been achieved. What are you thankful for? What are you proud of yourself for? Appreciate your own growth and resilience. Express gratitude for the journey you are on.

You can adapt these prompts to your personal style and experiences. Happy journaling!

Reflections
What are some key take aways for you?
_____
_____
_____
_____
_____

How will you use this information to support your approach to prayer practice?
_____
_____
_____
_____
_____
_____
_____
_____
_____
_____
_____
_____
_____

"If you believe in prayer at all, expect God to hear you. If you do not expect, you will not have. God will not hear you unless you believe He will hear you; but if you believe He will, He will be as good as your faith." - Charles Spurgeon

Motivation

Lord, please help me to remember that, sometimes growth and transformation come through challenges and discomfort. Help me to embrace the process, knowing that Your grace sustains me.

And this is the confidence that we have in him, that, if we ask any thing according to his will, he heareth us: and if we know that he hear us, whatsoever we ask, we know that we have the petitions that we desired of him. n

1 John 5:14
King James Version.

12

Further Reading and Resources

Delving deeper into the practice of journaling can significantly enrich your experience and understanding. In addition to the resources cited and referred to in the bibliography, here is a compilation of recommended books, articles, and online resources, along with supportive communities, workshops, and courses for continued learning and inspiration.

Recommended Books

- "The Artist's Way" by Julia Cameron: A foundational book that introduces "Morning Pages," a form of daily writing to unlock creativity.
- "Writing Down the Bones" by Natalie Goldberg: A guide that combines Zen teachings with practical writing advice.
- "The Bullet Journal Method" by Ryder Carroll: An exploration of the Bullet Journal system for organizing your life and thoughts.

Articles and Online Resources

- Articles on Mindful Journaling: Websites like Mindful.org and

Psychology Today often publish articles on the benefits and techniques of journaling.
- Journaling Blogs: Blogs such as "Journal Smarter" and "Tiny Buddha" offer tips, prompts, and inspiration for maintaining a journaling practice.

Supportive Communities

- Online Forums: Join forums such as Reddit's r/Journaling and r/BulletJournal for support, ideas, and community engagement.
- Social Media Groups: Facebook and Instagram have several groups and hashtags (e.g., #journalingcommunity) where people share their journaling journey and tips.

Workshops and Courses

- Mastermind.com: Explore courses and workshops offered by renowned experts like Tony Robbins and Dean Graziosi for in-depth learning.
- Udemy and Coursera: These platforms offer courses on creative writing, journaling for self-discovery, and more. Local Workshops: Check with local community centers, libraries, or bookstores for journaling workshops and meetups.

Continued Inspiration

- Journaling Prompts: Subscribe to websites that offer daily or weekly journaling prompts to keep your practice fresh and engaging.
- YouTube Channels: Channels dedicated to journaling, such as Boho Berry and Productive Journals, provide tutorials and inspiration through video content.

By exploring these resources, you can expand your knowledge of journaling, connect with supportive communities, and find ongoing inspiration to maintain and deepen your practice.

Reflection

Have you read a good book or found a good resource on journaling? Share your insights or list the resources here.

Expanded Journaling Prompts

Enhancing your journaling practice with specific themes can lead to more profound reflections and personal growth. In this chapter, we provide some enriched journaling prompts focused on prayer, testimony, and gratitude, along with themed prompts for different times of the year or spiritual milestones. By incorporating these prompts into your journaling practice, you can deepen your spiritual reflections and growth, aligning your daily writings with significant moments and themes in your faith journey.

The space provided in this book is for you to use to begin your own journaling practice.

Happy Journaling!

Happy journaling!

Prayer Prompts

Daily Prayer Reflection:
What are you thankful for today?

_____
_____
_____
_____
_____
_____
_____
_____

What do you seek guidance on?

_____
_____
_____
_____
_____
_____
_____
_____
_____

Intentions and Requests:
Write about the intentions you're holding in your heart, and the requests you want to lift in prayer.

_____
_____
_____
_____
_____
_____

Reflect on prayers that have been answered in your life and the impact they've had.

Personal Growth:

How has prayer influenced your personal growth and spiritual journey?

Communal Prayers:

Reflect on a prayer you've shared with a community or group. How did it affect your connection to others?

Testimony Prompts:

Spiritual Milestones:
Describe a significant spiritual milestone.

How did it shape your faith?

Witnessing Moments:

Reflect on a moment where you witnessed something profoundly spiritual.

_____
_____
_____
_____
_____
_____
_____
_____
_____

How did it impact you?

_____
_____
_____
_____
_____
_____

Sharing Your Story:
Write your testimony as if you were sharing it with someone seeking faith.

_____
_____
_____
_____
_____
_____
_____
_____

Influential Figures:
Who has influenced your spiritual journey?

Describe how they've impacted your faith.

Divine Encounters:
Recall a moment where you felt a divine presence.

How did it change your perspective or reinforce your beliefs?

Add Your Own Topics:

Gratitude Prompts:

Gratitude Lists:
Create a list of things you are grateful for today, highlighting both big and small blessings.

Gratitude Letters:
Write a letter of gratitude to someone who has made a significant impact on your life.

Gratitude in Challenges:

Reflect on a challenging time in your life. What lessons or hidden blessings emerged from it?

_____
_____
_____
_____
_____
_____
_____
_____
_____

Nature and Gratitude:

Describe how nature inspires feelings of gratitude in you.

_____
_____
_____
_____
_____
_____
_____
_____
_____

Daily Blessings:

Identify three blessings you've experienced today and explain why they are meaningful.

_____
_____
_____
_____
_____

Themed Prompts for Different Times of the Year

New Year

Resolution Prayers: What spiritual resolutions are you setting for the new year?

Reflecting on the Past Year: How has your faith grown over the past year?

What prayers were answered?

Easter

Resurrection Reflection: How does the resurrection story inspire your daily life?

Signs of New Life: Write about ways in which you see new beginnings or rebirth in your own life.

Thanksgiving

Harvest Gratitude: What are you harvesting in your life right now?

How do these blessings reflect God's goodness?

Acts of Kindness: Reflect on acts of kindness you've received and given. How do they embody gratitude?

Christmas

Gift of Faith: Reflect on the spiritual gifts you've received over the year.

Spirit of Giving: How does the spirit of Christmas inspire you to give to others, beyond material gifts?

Prompts for Specific Spiritual Milestones

Baptism

Baptismal Reflections: What does your baptism signify to you?

How has it shaped your faith journey?

The Practice of Journaling Prayer, Testimony, and Gratitude - 91

_____
_____
_____
_____
_____
_____
_____

Renewal of Vows: Reflect on any personal vows or commitments related to your baptism.
_____
_____
_____
_____
_____
_____
_____
_____

Confirmation
Holy Spirit's Role: How do you experience the presence of the Holy Spirit in your daily life?
_____
_____
_____
_____
_____
_____
_____
_____

Community Support: Write about the role community plays in your faith, especially during significant milestones like confirmation.

_____
_____
_____
_____
_____
_____
_____
_____
_____

Marriage

Spiritual Partnership: Reflect on your marriage as a spiritual journey. How do you support each other's faith?

_____
_____
_____
_____
_____
_____
_____
_____

Prayers for Union: Write prayers for your marriage, focusing on unity, love, and understanding.

_____
_____
_____
_____
_____
_____
_____

New Birth

Reflect on the anticipation: What were your thoughts and feelings leading up to the birth?

First meeting: Describe your emotions and experiences the first time you saw the newborn.

Future hopes and dreams: What do you hope for the future of this new life?

_____
_____
_____

Lessons from the journey: What have you learned about yourself through this experience?
_____
_____
_____
_____
_____
_____
_____
_____

New Engagement

Proposal moment: How did the proposal happen? Describe every detail you can remember.
_____
_____
_____
_____
_____
_____
_____
_____

Emotions on engagement: How do you feel about committing to this new journey?
_____
_____
_____

Shared dreams: What are your collective dreams and future plans?

Advice to your future self: What advice would you give yourself for the upcoming journey of marriage?

New Job or New Role
First impressions: What are your first thoughts about your new role and workplace?

New opportunities: What opportunities are you most excited about in this new job?

Goals and aspirations: What are your short-term and long-term goals in this new position?

Navigating challenges: How will you handle potential challenges in this new role?

Launch of a New Business

Vision and mission: Describe the vision and mission of your new business.

Describe the vision for your new business.

Describe the mission of your new business.

Initial journey: Reflect on the journey that led you to start this business.

Goals and milestones: What goals and milestones do you have for your business's first year?

Gratitude and support: Who has supported you along the way, and what are you most grateful for?

Add Your Own Topics:

Bibliography

1. Adele Ahlberg Calhoun 2015. Spiritual Disciplines Handbook: Practices That Transform Us. Revised and Expanded Edition
2. Kelli Mahoney 2019. Overview of Spiritual Disciplines and How They Work. Available at: https://www.learnreligions.com/what-are-spiritual-disciplines-712414 (Accessed: 22 May 2024).
3. Faith Practices Project 2024. What Is a Spiritual Discipline (Faith Practice)? Available at: https://www.crcna.org/FaithPracticesProject/what-spiritual-discipline-faith-practice (Accessed: 22 May 2024).
4. 9 Famous People Who Kept Journals - Develop Good Habits. Available at: https://www.developgoodhabits.com/famous-journals/. (Accessed: 22 May 2024).
5. How to Keep a Spiritual Journal like the Saints Did. Available at: https://pauline.org/Pauline-Books-Media-Blog/ArticleID/1395/How-to-Keep-a-Spiritual-Journal-like-the-Saints-Did. (Accessed: 22 May 2024).
6. John Burger (2021). These saints kept diaries - Aleteia. Available at: https://aleteia.org/2021/03/24/these-saints-kept-diaries/. (Accessed: 22 May 2024).
7. Real Men Journal, Too. - CBMW. Available at: https://cbmw.org/2013/10/11/real-men-journal-too/. (Accessed: 22 May 2024).
8. Sanjana Gupta 2023. The Importance of Self-Reflection: How Looking Inward Can Improve Your Mental Health. Available at: https://www.verywellmind.com/self-reflection-importance-benefits-and-strategies-7500858 (Accessed: 22 May 2024).
9. Spiritual Journaling: The Dos and Don'ts. Available at: https://www.thecatholicmag.com/spiritual-journaling-the-dos-donts/ (Accessed: 22 May 2024).
10. DHW Blog 2023. The Power of Journaling for Well-being: A Path to Self-Discovery and Healing - Available at: https://dhwblog.dukehealth.org/the-power-of-journaling-for-well-being-a-path-to-self-discovery-and-healing/ (Accessed: 22 May 2024).
11. Paul Brian 2023.The power of spiritual journaling: Techniques and

benefits. Available at: https://ideapod.com/spiritual-journaling/ (Accessed: 22 May 2024).

12. Journaling Scripture as a Spiritual Discipline - BibleGateway.com. Available at: https://www.biblegateway.com/resources/scripture-engagement/journaling-scripture/spiritual-discipline. (Accessed on June 8, 2024).

13. What is Spiritual Journaling and How to Get Started?. Available at: https://journling.com/what-is-spiritual-journaling/. (Accessed on June 8, 2024).

14. Patrick Oben Ministries. 2024. Ultimate Guide To Starting A Prayer Journal: Tips, Templates, And Transformative Practices. Available at: https://patrickoben.com/starting-prayer-journal-ultimate-guide/ (Accessed on June 8, 2024).

15. Phil Collins 2014. Journaling as a Spiritual Discipline. By Dr. Faye Chechowich, Taylor University. Materials adapted from Karen Mains Available at: https://www.biblegateway.com/resources/scripture-engagement/journaling-scripture/spiritual-discipline (Accessed on June 8, 2024).

16. Kelly O'Dell Stanley (2023). Why is prayer important? Available at: https://www.christianity.com/wiki/prayer/why-is-prayer-important.html (Accessed: 22 May 2024).

17. Bible verses related to The Importance Of Prayer from the King James Version (KJV) Available at: https://www.kingjamesbibleonline.org/Bible-Verses-About-The-Importance-Of-Prayer/ (Accessed: 22 May 2024).

18. Andy Reece (2024). The Importance of Prayer. 10 Reasons why w epray Available at: https://christian.net/resources/the-importance-of-prayer/ (Accessed: 22 May 2024).

19. Hilary Foye. What is prayer, and why should we pray? WordGo – Bible Study App Available at: https://www.wordgo.org/journal/what-is-prayer-and-why-should-we-pray (Accessed: 22 May 2024).

20. James Sandovalon (2023). What is Prayer According to the Bible? | Biblical Meaning (thebibleverses.org) Available at: https://thebibleverses.org/what-is-prayer/ (Accessed: 22 May 2024).

21. The Prayer Warrior (2024). Available at: https://thepraywarrior.com/35-proven-benefits-of-writing-down-prayers/ (Accessed: 22 May 2024).

22. Singh, M. (2018) If you feel thankful, write it down. it's good for your health, NPR. Available at: https://www.npr.org/sections/health-shots/2018/12/24/678232331/if-you-feel-thankful-write-it-down-its-good-for-your-health (Accessed: 22 May 2024).

23. Chowdhury, MR. (2019) The Neuroscience of Gratitude and Effects on the Brain. PositivePyschology.com. Available at: https://positivepsychology.com/neuroscience-of-gratitude/ (Accessed: 22 May 2024).

24. Pratt, M. (2022) The Science of Gratitude. Mindful: healthy mind, healthy life. Available at: https://www.mindful.org/the-science-of-gratitude/ (Accessed: 22 May 2024).

25. Kandler, M. (2018) What is a Gratitude Journal? Happyfeed. Available at: https://www.happyfeed.co/research/what-is-a-gratitude-journal (Accessed: 22 May 2024).

26. Cramoysan, S. (2021) The Benefits of Gratitude Journaling. The Positive Psychology People. Available at: https://www.thepositivepsychologypeople.com/the-benefits-of-gratitude-journaling/ (Accessed: 22 May 2024).

27. Singh, M. (2018) If you feel thankful, write it down. it's good for your health, NPR. Available at: https://www.npr.org/sections/health-shots/2018/12/24/678232331/if-you-feel-thankful-write-it-down-its-good-for-your-health (Accessed: 22 May 2024).

28. Kauffman, Marla (2023). The Power of Gratitude: A Scientific Look at How Thankfulness Boosts Mental Health. The Institute for Research, Education and Training in Addictions (IRETA). Published online December 20, 2023. Available at: The Power of Gratitude: A Scientific Look at How Thankfulness Boosts Mental Health - IRETA (Accessed 31 May 2024)

29. Kini P, Wong J, McInnis S, Gabana N, Brown JW. The effects of gratitude expression on neural activity. Neuroimage. 2016 Mar;128:1-10. doi: 10.1016/j.neuroimage.2015.12.040. Epub 2015 Dec 30. PMID: 26746580. (Accessed: 31 May 2024).

30. The Neuroscience of Gratitude: Rewiring Your Brain for Positivity. Available at: The Neuroscience of Gratitude: Rewiring Your Brain for Positivity (themindmender.net) (Accessed: 31 May 2024).

31. Emmons, Robert. (2018) The Psychology of Gratitude: Robert Emmons on How Saying Thanks Makes You Happier. Podcast recording on The Table Podcast. Biola University; Center for Christian Thought. Available at: https://cct.biola.edu/psychology-gratitude-robert-emmons-saying-thanks-makes-happier/ (Accessed: 31 May 2024).

32. Thanksgiving Prayer Examples. Bible Study Tools. Available at: https://www.biblestudytools.com/bible-study/topical-studies/thanksgiving-prayers-blessings-of-gratitude.html

33. Simple Sample of a Thanksgiving Prayer (learnreligions.com) Available at: https://www.learnreligions.com/thanksgiving-prayer-712346 (Accessed: 31 May 2024).

34. Prayer of Thanksgiving - God of all blessings, source of all life, giver (beliefnet.com) Available at: https://www.beliefnet.com/prayers/christian/gratitude/prayer-of-thanksgiving.aspx (Accessed: 31 May 2024).

35. 20 Prayers of Gratitude to Give Thanks to God. Available at: https://www.christianity.com/wiki/prayer/prayers-of-gratitude-to-give-thanks.html (Accessed: 31 May 2024).

36. 40 Thanksgiving Prayers and Blessings to Inspire Gratitude This Year (biblestudytools.com) Available at: https://www.biblestudytools.com/bible-

study/topical-studies/thanksgiving-prayers-blessings-of-gratitude.html (Accessed: 31 May 2024).

37. Bengtson, M. (2017). Testify to God's Goodness Available at: https://drmichellebengtson.com/testify-to-gods-goodness/ (Accessed: 22 May 2024).

38. Gray, Timberly (2014-2022). Do You Keep Track When God Answers Prayer? Available at: https://livingourpriorities.com/do-you-keep-track-of-your-answered-prayers/ (Accessed: 22 May 2024).

39. Timberley. Do You Keep Track When God Answers Prayer? Available at: https://livingourpriorities.com/do-you-keep-track-of-your-answered-prayers/ (Accessed: 19 June 2024).

40. Gina M Poirier. How to Start Prayer Journaling (With 20 Prompts for Women!) Available at: https://equippinggodlywomen.com/faith/prayer-journaling/ (Accessed: 19 June 2024).

41. Reflect on Growth: Observe how your prayers evolve and how God works in your life. Available at: https://equippinggodlywomen.com/faith/prayer-journaling/ (Accessed: 19 June 2024).

42. LaToya Edwards. The Ultimate Guide to Prayer Journaling for Beginners. Available at: https://latoyaedwards.net/how-to-make-a-prayer-journal/ (Accessed: 19 June 2024).

43. What To Do When Prayers Are Not Answered As A Christian? Available at: https://saintlyliving.com/prayer/what-to-do-when-prayers-are-not-answered/ (Accessed: 19 June 2024).

Other Books by Dr. Stephanie Fletcher-Lartey

Explore other titles written by Dr Stephanie Fletcher-Lartey on Book Distribution Platforms or visit her website at areteproconsult.com

www.ingramcontent.com/pod-product-compliance
Lightning Source LLC
Chambersburg PA
CBHW042043290426
44109CB00001B/17